Light and Color

Words by L. W. Anderson

Professor of Physics
University of Wisconsin—Madison

Raintree Childrens Books

Milwaukee

Cover Photo: Edmund Scientific Co.

Library of Congress Number: 87-23225

2 3 4 5 6 7 8 9 0 92 91 89 88

Printed and bound in the United States of America

Library of Congress Cataloging in Publication Data

Anderson, L. W. (Louis Wilmer), 1933-
  Light and color.

  Bibliography: p. 46
  Summary: Easy-to-read text and examples from daily
life introduce the concepts of light and color.
  1. Light—Juvenile literature.   2. Color—Juvenile
literature. [1. Light. 2. Color] I. Title.
QC360.A52 1987   535   87-23225
ISBN 0-8172-3257-5 (lib. bdg.)
ISBN 0-8172-3282-6 (softcover)

Light and
Color

Look around outside during the day. How many things can you see? Now look around the same place at night. How many things can you see now?

People need light to see. When light shines on things, some of the light bounces off and into our eyes. This is how we see. If light does not shine on something, we cannot see it.

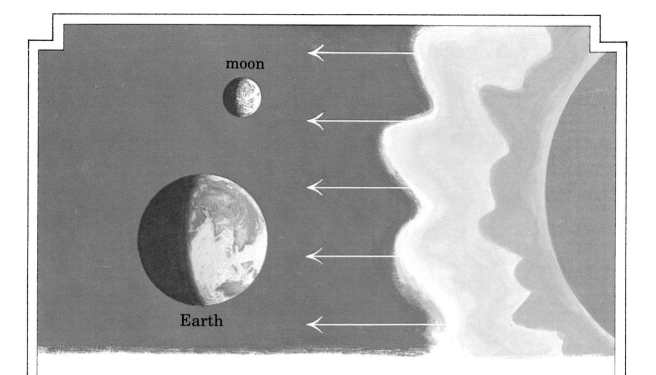

The sun shines on the earth and the moon. The moon does not make light. We see sunlight that bounces off the moon. If you were on the moon, the earth would seem to shine. You would be seeing the sunlight that bounces off the earth.

We can describe
how light works.
Throw a stone into
water. It will send out
waves. Light moves in
waves like this.

Point a flashlight
at the ceiling. The
light goes straight to
the ceiling. Light
waves move in a
straight line.

A straight path of light is called a ray. Rays of light go through glass and water. But glass and water bend light when it goes in and when it comes out.

The ruler and the pencil look bent in the water. This is because the light bouncing off them has been bent. The bending of light is called refraction.

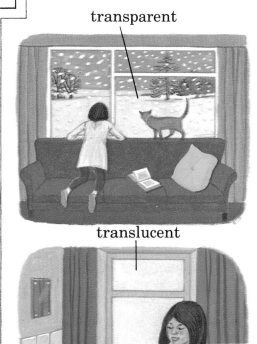

transparent

translucent

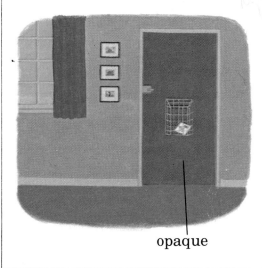

opaque

Light goes through clear glass. You can see through this glass window. When you can see clearly through something, it is called transparent.

Some things let light through, but you cannot see clearly through them. These are called translucent.

Some things do not let light come through at all. You cannot see through them. Things that stop light are called opaque.

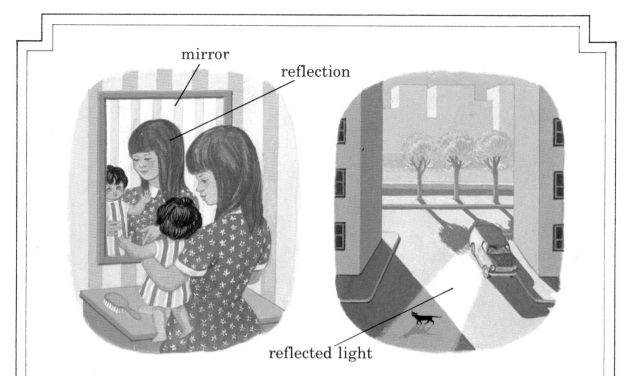

mirror

reflection

reflected light

When light bounces off something, we say that the light is reflected. You can see yourself in a mirror. This is because light bounces off you to the mirror and back to your eyes. A mirror reflection reverses right and left. If you wave your right hand, your reflection seems to wave the left hand.

Shiny things reflect light. When light hits a shiny object, it bounces off in the opposite direction. This is why the van reflects the light in the opposite direction.

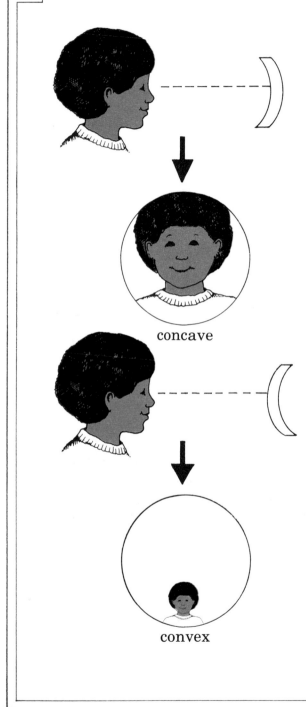

concave

convex

Some mirrors curve in, like the inside of a bowl. They are called concave. A concave mirror can be used as a magnifier.

Some mirrors curve out, like the outside of a bowl. These are called convex. A convex mirror makes things look smaller than they are. Some mirrors on cars and trucks are convex.

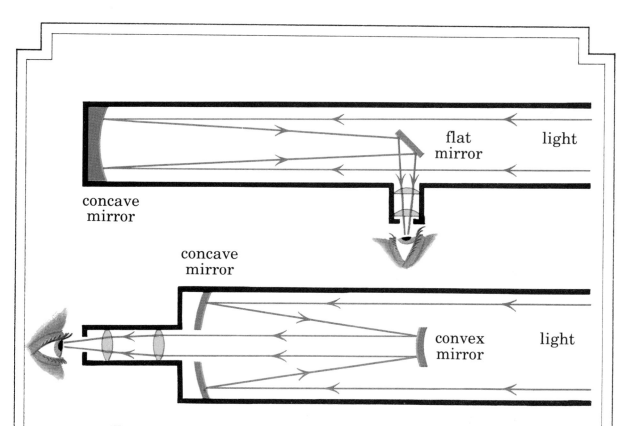

Telescopes use specially shaped mirrors. We use telescopes to make distant things look larger. We point the telescope at the thing we want to see. Light from that thing enters one end of the telescope. It reflects off the mirrors. The last mirror reflects the light out to the eye.

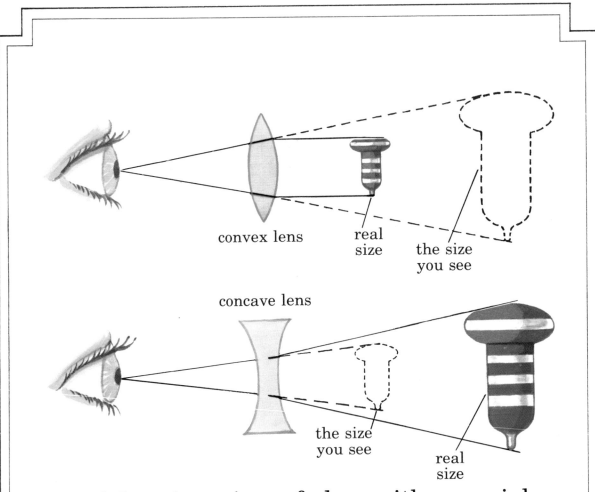

convex lens

real size

the size you see

concave lens

the size you see

real size

A lens is a piece of glass with a special shape. Lenses bend light as it passes through them. A convex lens can make the things you look at seem bigger. A concave lens can make things seem smaller.

eyeglasses

magnifying glass

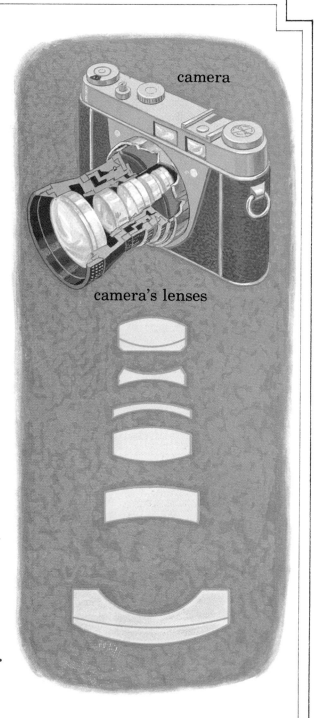

camera

camera's lenses

Lenses can be used in many ways. They are used in eyeglasses to help people see clearly. They are used in magnifying glasses to make things look bigger. Lenses are also used in cameras.

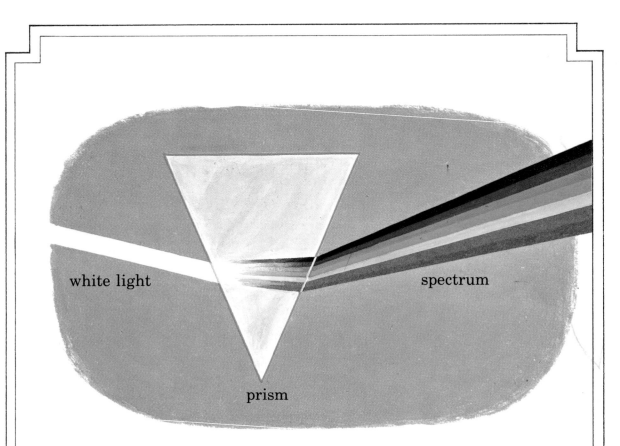

white light

spectrum

prism

Most light looks white. But if you shine light through a specially shaped glass called a prism, the light breaks into different colors. White light is made from these colors. The different colors include red, orange, yellow, green, blue, indigo, and violet. The colors are called the spectrum.

The girl colors
the cardboard circle
with seven colors
of the spectrum.

Then she spins it
around fast. The
colors mix together
to look white.

rainbow

A rainbow is a spectrum. It is made when light goes through drops of water. The drops of water act similar to the way prisms do. They break up the light into the colors of the spectrum.

Some kinds of light cannot be seen by people. One kind is at the farthest violet end of the spectrum. We call it ultraviolet light. Ultraviolet light is what gives you sunburn.

At the farthest red end of the spectrum is infrared light. We use it to take pictures at night. Special cameras can use infrared light when everything seems dark to human eyes.

badger at night

An object looks a certain color because it reflects that color from the spectrum. It takes in, or absorbs, all other colors. Something looks red because it reflects red and absorbs all other colors. Purple is made from red and blue put together. Something looks purple because it reflects red and blue from the spectrum.

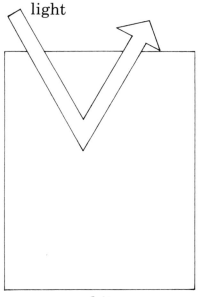

white
all light reflected

black
all light absorbed

White things reflect all colors which make up white light. No colors are absorbed. Black things absorb all the colors of white light. No colors are reflected.

Red, green, and blue can be used as the three *primary* colors of light. All other colors of light can be made from these three.

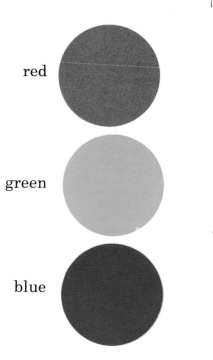

red

green

blue

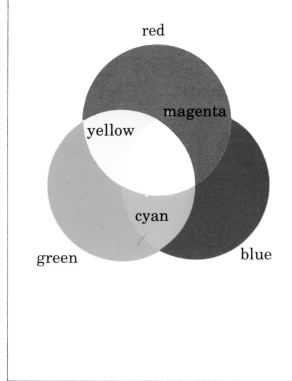

Green and blue make a color called cyan. Blue and red make magenta. Red and green make yellow. Red, green, and blue light together make white light.

If you shine a colored light on something white, it will appear that color. The clown looks red in red light. Red and green lights mix to make yellow light. The clown looks yellow in that light. The primary colors red, green, and blue mix to make white. When these lights mix, the clown looks white again.

For every color of light there is an opposite, or complementary, color. The two colors together make white. Blue and yellow are complementary colors of light.

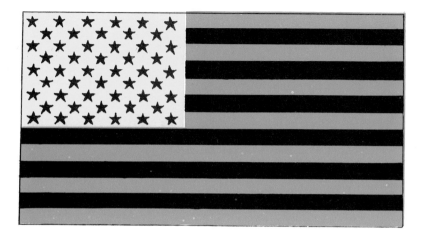

Look at a color for a long time. Now look at something white. You will see a color that is complementary to the color of the first thing you were looking at. This is because your eyes get fatigued for the first color.

Look at this flag for about one minute under a bright light. Now look at white paper. You should see the American flag in its correct colors.

The primary colors
of paint are often
taken to be different
from red, green, and
blue. Paints absorb
some colors and reflect
others. The primary
colors of paint are
often taken as yellow,
magenta, and cyan.

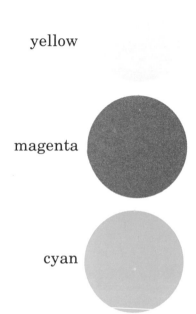

yellow

magenta

cyan

We can make all
the other colors of
paint using these
three colors. When all
three primary colors of
paint are mixed
together, the paint
looks black.

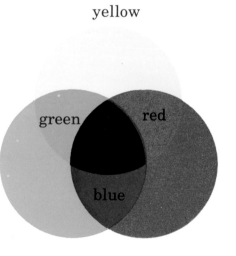

yellow

green

red

blue

A painter can make all colors from three primary ones. To make green, he mixes cyan and yellow. If he wants black, he can mix all three colors together.

People made the
first paints from
rocks and clay. They
painted pictures with
these paints in their
caves. We can still
see some of the
pictures today.

Paints can be used to color cloth. These paints are called dyes. People used to color cloth by stirring it in a tub of dye. They had only a few colors. Now we have machines that dye cloth. Most dyes today are made from petroleum. The dyes can be made any color people want.

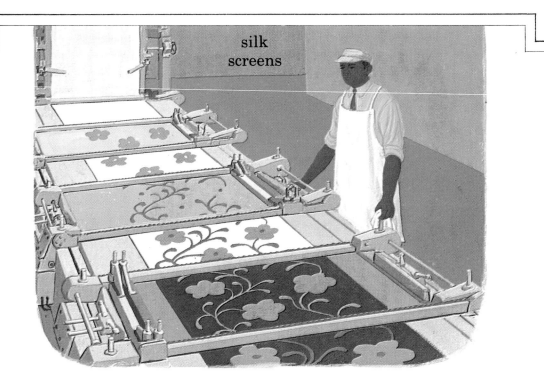

silk
screens

   People use dyes to print patterns on cloth. One way of doing this is called silk screening. Silk is stretched across frames. When there is a lot of cloth to print, the frames are on a big machine.

Each silk screen
prints a different
color and shape. The
cloth moves along
under the silk screens.
It comes out with
the entire colored
pattern.

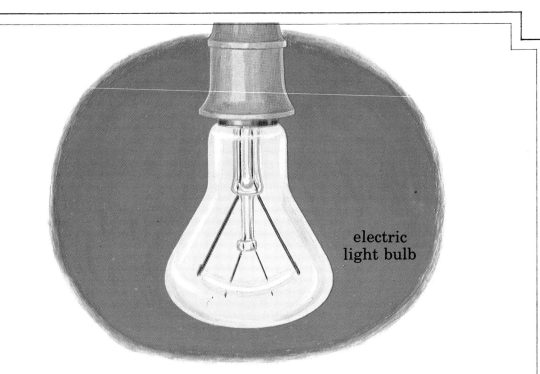

electric
light bulb

When it is dark we can make light.
Most people use electric lights. Electric
lights for the home have glass bulbs. Inside
the bulb there is a thin wire. The wire
shines brightly when electric current goes
through it.

glowworm

phosphorescent rock

Some animals can make their own light. A glowworm is a kind of beetle. Light shines from its abdomen.

Some plants and rocks can glow with their own light. This kind of light is called phosphorescence.

The light from these living things gives off very little heat.

Some animals use color to protect themselves. The moth is the same color as the tree trunk it is resting on. Chameleons change their color to match the things around them. Enemies of the moth and chameleon have a hard time finding them.

moth

tree trunk

chameleon

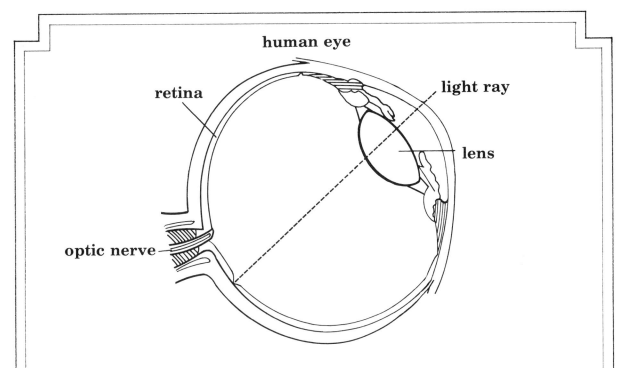

human eye

retina

light ray

lens

optic nerve

We can see because of our eyes and our brain. Light rays enter the eye and pass through its lens. The lens bends the light rays so that they land on the retina. The retina is a layer of cells that covers the back of the eye. There are special cells in the retina that "see" light and color. These cells send messages to the brain along the optic nerve. The brain puts together the messages from the eye to tell us what we are seeing.

The Metric System

In the United States, things are measured in inches, pounds, quarts, and so on. That system is called the American system. Most other countries of the world use centimeters, kilograms, and liters to measure those things. That system is called the metric system.

At one time the United States was going to change to the metric system. That is why you will see both systems of measurement in some books. For example, you might see a sentence like this: "That bicycle wheel is 27 inches (69 centimeters) across."

Most books you use will have only one system of measurement. You may want to change from one system to the other. The chart on the next page will help you.

All you have to do is multiply the unit of measurement in Column 1 by the number in Column 2. Your answer will be the unit in Column 3.

Suppose you want to change 15 centimeters to inches. First, find *centimeters* in Column 1. Next, multiply 15 times .4. The answer you get is 6. So, 15 centimeters equal 6 inches.

Column 1	Column 2	Column 3
THIS UNIT OF MEASUREMENT	TIMES THIS NUMBER	GIVES THIS UNIT OF MEASUREMENT
inches	2.54	centimeters
feet	30.	centimeters
feet	.3	meters
yards	.9	meters
miles	1.6	kilometers
ounces	28.	grams
pounds	.45	kilograms
fluid ounces	.03	liters
pints	.47	liters
quarts	.95	liters
gallons	3.8	liters
centimeters	.4	inches
meters	1.1	yards
kilometers	.6	miles
grams	.035	ounces
kilograms	2.2	pounds
liters	33.8	fluid ounces
liters	2.1	pints
liters	1.06	quarts
liters	.26	gallons

Where to Read About
Light and Color

Pronunciation Key

a	a as in **cat, bad**
ā	a as in **able**, ai as in **train**, ay as in **play**
ä	a as in **father, car**, o as in **cot**
e	e as in **bend, yet**
ē	e as in **me**, ee as in **feel**, ea as in **beat**, ie as in **piece**, y as in **heavy**
i	i as in **in, pig**, e as in **pocket**
ī	i as in **ice, time**, ie as in **tie**, y as in **my**
o	o as in **top**, a as in **watch**
ō	o as in **old**, oa as in **goat**, ow as in **slow**, oe as in **toe**
ô	o as in **cloth**, au as in **caught**, aw as in **paw**, a as in **all**
oo	oo as in **good**, u as in **put**
o͞o	oo as in **tool**, ue as in **blue**
oi	oi as in **oil**, oy as in **toy**
ou	ou as in **out**, ow as in **plow**
u	u as in **up, gun**, o as in **other**
ur	ur as in **fur**, er as in **person**, ir as in **bird**, or as in **work**
yo͞o	u as in **use**, ew as in **few**
ə	a as in **again**, e as in **broken**, i as in **pencil**, o as in **attention**, u as in **surprise**
ch	ch as in **such**
ng	ng as in **sing**
sh	sh as in **shell, wish**
th	th as in **three, bath**
<u>th</u>	th as in **that, together**

GLOSSARY

abdomen (ab′ də mən) the rear part of an insect's body

absorb (ab sôrb′) to take in; soak up

beetle (bēt′ əl) an insect with hard wings

bounce (bouns) to hit something and spring back

bowl (bōl) a curved, rounded dish used to hold things

brain (brān) the organ inside the head that thinks, learns, and controls the body

bulb (bulb) the thin, rounded glass part of an electric light

camera (kam′ ər ə) something that is used to take photographs

cardboard (kärd′ bôrd) a thick, stiff paper, often used in boxes

cave (kāv) a large hole in the ground or the side of a hill

ceiling (sē′ ling) the top of a room

cell (sel) a small, basic unit of living matter

chameleon (kə mēl′ yən) a lizard that can change the color of its skin

clay (klā) a kind of earth that is easy to shape

clear (klēr) letting light through; easy to see through

coal tar (kōl tär) a dark, sticky liquid made from coal

complementary (kom plə ment′ ə rē) acting as one of a pair of colors that make white or black when put together

concave (kon kāv′) curving inward

convex (kon veks′) curving outward

correct (kə rekt′) having no mistakes

curve (kurv) to move in a rounded line; to bend in one direction

cyan (sī′ ən) a green blue color; one of the primary colors of paint

dye (dī) a substance used to color cloth or other things

electric (i lek′ trik) being run by electricity

electricity (i lek tris′ ə tē) a basic form of energy; electric current

eyeglasses (ī′ glas′ iz) lenses in a frame that people wear to help them see

flashlight (flash′ līt′) a small electric light that can be carried in the hand

glowworm (glō′ wərm) a beetle that shines light from its body

heat (hēt) warmth; the state of being hot

human (hyoo′ mən) having to do with people

indigo (in′ di go′) a dark blue color

infrared (in′ frə red′) a color that we can't see that is at the farthest red end of the spectrum

inward (in′ wərd) moving toward the inside

lens (lenz) a curved piece of glass that bends light in a certain way

magenta (mə jent′ ə) a blue red color; one of the primary colors of paint

magnifying glass (mag′ nə fī′ ing   glas) a
  lens which makes things look bigger
mirror (mir′ ər) a shiny object which
  reflects the light from things in
  front of it
mixture (miks′ chər) different things
  put together
moon (mo͞on) the large body that circles
  the earth
moth (môth) an insect with wings that
  usually flies at night
object (ob′ jikt) a thing; something you
  can see and touch
opaque (ō pāk′) not letting light through;
  not transparent or translucent
opposite (op′ ə zit) completely different;
  on the other side or across from something
optic nerve (op′ tik   nurv) an important
  nerve that connects the eye and the brain
outward (out′ wərd) going toward the outside
pattern (pat′ ərn) a certain order of
  colors or shapes

pencil (pen′ səl) a long, thin object
  used for writing

phosphorescence (fäs′ fə res′ əns) a kind
  of light that comes from animals or rocks

photograph (fō′ tə graf) a picture
  taken by a camera

primary (prī′ mer ē) being important or
  a main thing

print (print) to put pictures or letters
  on some surface

prism (priz′ əm) a clear object with flat
  sides that breaks up light into a spectrum

purple (pur′ pəl) a color that is a
  mixture of red and blue

rainbow (rān′ bō′) a curving band of
  colors in the air

ray (rā) a narrow path of light

react (rē akt′) to act because of
  something else that has happened

reflect (ri flekt′) to send or bounce back

reflection (ri flek′ shən) the image seen
  in a reflecting surface

refraction (ri frak′ shən) the bending
   of light as it goes in and comes out
   of something
retina (ret′ ən ə) the light-sensitive
   lining at the back of the eyeball
reverse (ri vurs′) to turn something
   around to the opposite position
screen (skrēn) a net or mesh stretched
   on a frame
silk (silk) a soft, fine cloth made
   from threads spun by silkworms
skin (skin) the outer covering of the
   body
spectrum (spek′ trəm) the colors that
   make up white light
spin (spin) to turn around and around
   quickly
stir (stur) to move something
   around and around
sunlight (sun′ līt′) the light from the sun
telescope (tel′ ə skōp′) something that
   makes far things look closer

translucent (trans loo′ sənt) letting
light pass through

transparent (trans per′ ənt) clear;
letting light through so things on
the other side can be seen

tub (tub) a large, round, open container

ultraviolet (əl′ trə vī′ ə lit) a color that
we cannot see, at the farthest violet end
of the spectrum

van (van) a covered truck used to move
large things

violet (vī′ ə lit) a soft blue purple color

Bibliography

Broekel, Ray. *Experiments with Light.*
Chicago: Childrens Press, 1986.

Freeman, Tony. *Photography.* Chicago:
Childrens Press, 1983.

Iveson, Joan. *Your Eyes.* New York:
Bookwright Press, 1985.

Seymore, Peter. *Colors.* New York:
Macmillan, 1984.

Simon, Hilda. *The Magic of Color.* New
York: Lothrop, Lee, and Shepard, 1981.

Simon, Seymore. *Mirror Magic.* New York:
Lothrop, Lee, and Shepard, 1980.

Wilkin, Fred. *Microscopes and Telescopes.*
Chicago: Childrens Press, 1983.

Yajima, Minoru. *The Firefly.* Milwaukee:
Raintree Publishers, 1986.